Dreams in Captivity

A Play in Two Acts

by

Gabriel Davis

gabriel@alumni.cmu.edu
gabrielbdavis.com
Registered WGA

Characters

Paxton Prichard
a chef

Livi James
care aid in a nursing home

Barry James
her brother, a salesman

Reina James
his wife, a mother

Place
a small city

Time
the present

ACT ONE

SCENE 1:

(Staff lounge in a retirement home)

(Livi enters, stopping at the entrance. She wears scrubs).

> LIVI
> (Speaking to someone just beyond the entrance)
> No, Mr. Fine, I'm still on my break. Let me just...Let me just grab some coffee – go to your room – I promise I'll be in to give you your insulin in just a minute. Just one minute. Okay?
> (She moves into the room, looking tired. Rubs her forehead. Pours herself coffee, tastes   it, grimaces. She leans on the table, which holds the coffee machine just breathing, trying   to relax. Then she roots around in a sugar bowl, looking for sugar packet among a bunch   of Sweet 'n Low packets).
> Sugar. Sugar. Sugar. Where are you?

> (Pax enters. Livi's back is to him).

> PAX
> (calling off)
> Just sit there and relax, Grandma. I think there's some coffee in here.
> (to Livi)
> Excuse me. Would you mind if I...
> (Livi turns to face him)

> LIVI
> Can I help you with something?

> (Pause)

> PAX
> Livi James? Livi James. My God, is it really you?

> LIVI
> Do I know—

> PAX
> Livi it's *me.* Pax.

> LIVI
> Pax...?

> PAX
> Paxton Prichard. From high school.

                    LIVI

Oh. Oh! Yes, yes, Pax. Pax. I'm sorry... You look so—. Your hair's—

                    PAX

Chopped off. Yeah. You look fantastic.

                    LIVI

Oh no.

                    PAX

So you work here?

                    LIVI

Thus the flattering attire.

                    PAX

On you, it works.

                    LIVI

Did you want something?

                    PAX

Yeah, I'm sorry, I know the door said "Staff Only," but my grandma
wanted some coffee and—

                    LIVI

It's okay. She take sugar?

                    PAX

Black is fine.

                    LIVI

So is your grandmother moving in here?

                    PAX

We're still in the considering phase. Whatever she decides. It's great to
see you again. I can't get over this. Livi James. How are you?

                    LIVI

I'm okay. You?

                    PAX

Fantastic.

                    LIVI

Well, here's the coffee.

                    PAX

I can't tell you how really *nice* it is to see you.

4

                              LIVI
You too.
         (Looking at her watch)
Oh shoot.

                              PAX
What?

                              LIVI
I have to give one of the residents his...breaks go fast here. I'm sorry.
I would. I really would like to catch up but...well, it was nice seeing you
again, Pax.

         (Livi heads for the door)

                              PAX
You know, I thought you'd be in New York or L.A. for sure by now.
         (Livi stops, turns)

                              LIVI
Why's that?

                              PAX
Are you kidding? *Everyone* thought you'd be—I mean, you were
incredible in *The Sound of Music.*

                              LIVI
That was high school.

                              PAX
(continuous) The way the auditorium would get when you'd take the
stage. I mean, you like *tamed* all those adolescent *animals*. And it was
only you. For everyone else, it was catcalling and snickering and
mumbling and crinkling of programs. You came out on that stage.
Silence. Absolute focus. Every eye on you.

                              LIVI
Yeah well...now I keep my eye on others.

                              PAX
Can I ask what happened?

                              LIVI
I applied to acting schools and everything. Even got in. One of the
good ones.

                              PAX
That's great. And now you're...here...?

                              LIVI
I really should get back.

                              PAX
Can I have a little sugar first, for my grandma's coffee.

                              LIVI
Oh. Okay. I'm not sure we...
          (She rummages through, looking for sugar)

                              PAX
          (reaching in to take a Sweet 'n Low)
Sweet 'n Low's fine.
          (He takes it, she quickly grabs it away from him)

                              LIVI
Don't use that.

                              PAX
Why not?

                              LIVI
Cancer. In rats.

                              PAX
Pardon?

                              LIVI
You know, the experiments. They found Sweet 'n Low causes –

                              PAX
Isn't that only if you like consume massive amounts of it?

                              LIVI
(continuous over the above) – tumors in lab rats. I keep telling our
supervisor to stop keeping it in here. I tell him. Life's too short to take
those kind of risks. Over a few calories. Right? Wait. There's got to be
a few real sugars buried in here somewhere. I've been looking but...
Here we go! Sugar in the Raw. Last one.
          (She looks at it for a moment. Then gives it to him)

                              PAX
Thanks. So you've trained as an actor then?

                              LIVI
No. Look, I really should—

                              PAX

___
6

Really? You didn't—

                              LIVI
I really have to—
         (She moves toward the door)

                              PAX
Oh. Okay.

                              LIVI
It's just that one of the residents needs his insulin...and anyway, you
don't want to hear about—

                              PAX
I *do. Genuinely.*

         (Livi considers going, then takes a step toward Pax instead)

                              LIVI
After graduation I took this as a summer job, you know.   Just
transitional. But there were so many people here who needed tending.
It was understaffed. Still is. And this one man, Mr. Fine. I went to
clean him. His back was all covered in...it was like sweat and caked in
dirt...

                              PAX
(realizes) They weren't washing him.

                              LIVI
We're always losing Care Aids here. The pay isn't high enough. People
get overlooked. It felt good to make sure Mr. Fine was comfortable.
And when it came time to go...I just felt like maybe...

                              PAX
You should stay?

                              LIVI
People here needed me.

                              PAX
Can I ask...which school did you get into?

                              LIVI
Julliard.

         (Beat)

                              PAX

You think it's possible for me to bring my grandma back for another visit? I mean...*you* lead visits ever?

                              LIVI
No, but I'm taking some of the residents on a trip to the zoo.

                              PAX
Oh that's great. The zoo! I love—my *grandma* loves animals.

SCENE 2:

(The Zoo)

(Sound of monkeys. Pax enters)

                              PAX
No no, you stay with the group, Grandma. Livi, come here, I want you to see this.

                              LIVI
          (off)
I can't! I have to stay with the group.

                              PAX
They'll be fine. You gotta see this! C'mon!

                              LIVI
What is so important—

                              PAX
Look at them!

                              LIVI
Cute little things.

                              PAX
Look at how they leap between branches. Effortless, fearless, no regard for gravity. Like it doesn't *apply* to *them*. They're practically flying. Looks how I feel today.

                              LIVI
When I was little I used to climb in trees. To get away from my brother.

                              PAX
Oh. Right. *Barry.*

                              LIVI
Yeah, *Barry.*

8

                              PAX
He taunted you pretty regularly, huh?

                              LIVI
You'd know about regular tauntings, right? With your older brother...?

                              PAX
Bret. No. Not really. He pretty much protected me.

     (Awkward silence)

                              LIVI
Your grandmother seems to be enjoying herself.

                              PAX
Well, like I said, she *loves* animals.

     (Awkward silence)

                              LIVI
It can be a nightmare. Doing meals during these field trips. Did you see
the way I had to wrestle Mr. Fine when he bought that ice-cream
sandwich?

                              PAX
Mr. Fine loved the wrestling, Livi. He had this big smile on his face. I'd
have the same smile.

                              LIVI
He's *diabetic*. Ice cream could kill him. So what's your story anyway?
Just back from college or...?

                              PAX
Didn't finish.

                              LIVI
Oh?

                              PAX
Three years in, I just couldn't see the point. I started to feel I was there
because I *had* to. Because it was *expected*.

                              LIVI
Hm.

                              PAX

It's a funny story. I decided to withdraw from classes. My parents decided to cut me off. I ran out of money and took up residence on my buddy's sofa. So there I was, feeling kinda lost, directionless, living off his Mac 'n Cheese and Ramen noodles. And I start dreaming up all these dishes I could cook. And my buddy's always getting high, and I'm always telling him my food ideas. Finally, it's more than he can take, he goes out and *shops* for the ingredients. I make him these thin slices of soy-marinated steak. Flash seared so it's rare in the middle. I roll it around an avocado, cucumber salad. He loves it. Word spreads. Soon I'm cooking for all our friends. I'm booked days in advance. And I think, hey. This is good. This I can do. So I decide to enroll in this culinary school...

                    LIVI
You have a culinary degree?

                    PAX
Not exactly. Look at these monkeys. They're great. They get it. Ya know. How to just, really dig in and enjoy life. Look at 'em. All naked and happy. Look at that one. Oh wow. He's interesting. Come here. Check him out up close. C'mon.
          (Livi comes close, looking at him, fascinated)
He likes you, I guess.

                    LIVI
Oh...God. Don't try to hide their feelings, do they?

                    PAX
It's animal instinct, Livi – he sees something beautiful, he responds.

                    LIVI
Isn't he the kind of monkey that spread Ebola?

                    PAX
No, that's Capuchin. He's a Rhesus Monkey, same kind they sent adventuring into space.

          (beat. Livi eyes the monkey for a moment. Then back to Pax)

                    LIVI
So you're still in culinary school?

                    PAX
No. Culinary school cramped my style. No room for originality.

                    LIVI
Oh. So what are you doing now?   Working...?

                    PAX

___

Nah. Staying at my parents' house. Just for now. Just for the time being.
      (coming close, conspiratorial)
Look, can I go out on a limb here?

               LIVI
Like the monkeys?

               PAX
Seeing you again has made me feel so...

               LIVI
Yeah...?

               PAX
Well...a lot of things...but also, *motivated.* I mean, being with you – suddenly I feel I can just...

               LIVI
What?

               PAX
So I don't have a culinary degree? So what? Right? I mean, I have a spark for this. And seeing you – it's like that spark has caught fire and – and I really feel I have something to offer...the *world* as a cook. I mean, I think – I think I really want to start my own restaurant! Do I sound crazy?

               LIVI
Paxton Prichard. No, not crazy...cute. You wanna maybe get dinner sometime?

               PAX
How about I *make* it. *Tonight.*

SCENE 3:

(Livi's apartment)

(Livi stares at her piece of tuna steak. Pax is devouring his.)

               PAX
Mmmm. Oh God. Mmmm. Jesus. Jesus. Oh. Oh. Yeah.
      (He takes his plate up to scrape any last little bit directly into
      this mouth. He's finished, looking up)
I'm sorry. I just got so deep into it. My cooking tonight was...you really inspired me.

                    LIVI

Really?

                    PAX

Really. You not hungry?

                    LIVI

Pardon?

                    PAX

You haven't *touched* your tuna steak.

                    LIVI

Well...

                    PAX

Do you not like Thai spices?

                    LIVI

No, I mean, I've never... I was wondering. What is that wonderful
smell?

                    PAX

Oh, a citrus-ginger glaze I make with—

                    LIVI

No, it's coming from... I mean. This smells nice. Mmm. But. There's
this smell. I think it's coming from...you... Do you mind if I?

        (Livi gets up and moves toward Pax)

                    PAX

Um, no—

                    LIVI

What is that?

                    PAX

Drakkar Noir?

                    LIVI

No. No. No that's just a slight *tinge*...
        (Takes a deep breath)
Mothballs?
        (Takes another deep breath in the right spot)
Yep. Mothballs.

                    PAX

Oh, well, I spent the day at my Grandmother's house and then...I'm
sorry...

                         LIVI
I like it. It's comforting. Familiar.

                         PAX
I like it too.
          (beat)
So are you going to try my –

                         LIVI
Thanks so much for doing all this.

                         PAX
Oh. Sure. Thanks for letting me use your kitchen. I would have made
it at my parents' place but Dad's throwing a dinner party. Some snob-
fest. You not like tuna?

                         LIVI
Oh no, I love tuna.

                         PAX
Oh good.

                         LIVI
Looks great. Very visually, ah, *vibrant.*
          (Takes a sip of the wine)
Great wine.

                         PAX
It's shit. It's *Catawba.* The tuna is really the thing that—

                         LIVI
It's just...it looks so artistic, I'm afraid to...

                         PAX
It's art meant to be devoured. Go on.

          (Long pause)

                         LIVI
It's not cooked? I mean. All the way?

                         PAX
It's raw in the middle. Seared on the outside. Best like that.

                         LIVI
Is that *safe*? Being raw?

                              PAX
It's fresh. It's *Ahi*.

                              LIVI
Expensive?

                              PAX
Why do you think we're drinking *Catawba*? *Try* it.

                              LIVI
You mind if I put some ketchup on—

                              PAX
Can't put ketchup on that.

                              LIVI
I put ketchup on everything.

                              PAX
Everything?
        (Livi nods)
Try this as is. Trust me. You'll be swooning.

                              LIVI
From illness? Kidding. Ha. Ha. What? I'm kidding. You look offended.

                              PAX
This is what I do for a living.

                              LIVI
Aren't you unemployed? Ha ha. Kidding. I'm *kidding*.

                              PAX
I put my heart into cooking this!

                              LIVI
Doesn't look cooked to me. Ha ha, ha ha, ha ha—. C'mon. *Laugh.*
Please?
        (Pax gets up from the table and throws himself on the floor)
What's wrong? Talk to me. Are you okay? Hello?

                              PAX
        (Lying prone)
This is my life. Oh God. You don't trust my *cooking*.

                              LIVI
I was only—

___
14

PAX

My father's right. He thinks I'm bound for failure. He says if I can't inspire confidence in others that I can *do* this....

LIVI

This is pretty heavy stuff for a first date, Pax.

PAX

I know, I'm sorry—

LIVI

It's *okay* ..

PAX

He just – it's like he only *sees* me when I'm doing something he can brag to his friends about—

LIVI

At least he *sees* you.

PAX

What do you mean?

LIVI

Okay – my first memory – I mean, literally the first thing I can remember about my dad. Barry's got me pinned down and he's letting a little bit of spit slowly fall out of his mouth, then sucking it back up, before it falls. I remember my dad walked by. I mean, he *saw*.
        (beat)
He just *walked by.*
        (beat)
After Dad died, Barry told me he was different...before Mom... I was too young to remember her. She met the guy she ran off with when she was still pregnant with me. Some friend she'd take to her Lamaze classes when Dad couldn't make it.
        (Pax touches her face. They share a smile, but then an
        awkwardness sets in).

PAX

Listen...let's go back over...eat the—

LIVI

Can I microwave it?

PAX

It's so good raw inside. It's like sushi.

LIVI

I've never had that.

PAX

Just a taste then. *Believe* in this amazing bite.

LIVI

What's the big deal if *I* believe in "this amazing bite"?

PAX

Because it's *you*. *Livi James.*

LIVI

Look...your, your *friends* loved your food in college, right? What about that?

(Pax, being playful, starts to feign anger)

PAX

They were all high. They had the munchies. They'd probably have loved ANYTHING. You're like, the first sober person …

LIVI

I doubt that.

PAX

… and you – YOU WON'T EVEN TRY MY FOOD!

LIVI

This is babyish. This is like a tantrum.

PAX

THIS IS A TANTRUM! I'M THROWING A TANTRUM! TRY MY TUNA!

LIVI

BEHAVE YOU NAUGHTY LITTLE CHEF!

(Beat, Pax goes and gets the tuna, and approaches Livi with it, the following is a playful, mutual approach: they get closer with each line)

PAX

I like you. You put up with me.

LIVI

Everyday, I deal with worse. At the home.

PAX

Really?

LIVI

The de-maturation process of ageing.

                              PAX
De-maturation. Nice. Not a word. But nice.

                              LIVI
Old men, like adolescent schoolboys.

                              PAX
Senility.

                              LIVI
Mortality.

                              PAX
Sex and death.

                              LIVI
They go hand in hand.

                              PAX
A final, desperate urge to procreate.
          (Pax holds the tuna between them)

                              LIVI
The penis's last cry in the face of the endless void.

                              PAX
Standing bravely.

                              LIVI
Ultimately alone.
          (They're very close now)

                              PAX
Your tuna?

                              LIVI
          (Livi sits on the couch)
I showed a dying man my breasts once.

                              PAX
What?

                              LIVI
          (Livi begins unbuttoning her blouse)
He asked. And I thought. What's the difference? He won't *tell* anyone.
No one will *know*. Put down the tuna.

                              PAX
Full disclosure. I'm not dying.

                              LIVI
We're all dying.

                              PAX
This bite of tuna is to die for …

                              LIVI
          (She takes the tuna and puts it down, moving closer to Pax)
Forget about the tuna.
          (Livi kisses Pax, he kisses back. Slow fade to black)

SCENE 4:

(Livi and Pax's Apartment)

(Reina enters with boxes, Livi takes a box from Reina. Reina moves into
living room and puts her box down. Livi stays at the door)

                              REINA
I just can't understand it. I mean...put yourself in my shoes for a
minute. Your sister-in-law calls you up and says, "Guess what?
Surprise, I'm married."

                              LIVI
I know, to you, it seemed sudden but...
          (Calling out the door)
Pax, you sure you don't need us to carry any more of those boxes?

                              PAX
          (offstage)
No. I'm fine!

                              LIVI
But it's not *totally* sudden. I mean, he's pretty much been staying here
every night the last month—

                              REINA
Still, only a *month*?

                              LIVI
It feels like an eternity has passed between us in that time.

                              REINA
It does?

                    LIVI
It's been amazing.

                    REINA
It has?

                    LIVI
Yes.

                    REINA
Still, I don't know. There was this article in *Woman Magazine* about
women who elope—they say it can be a sign of deep-seated
insecurities...

                    LIVI
Do you want to hear how he—?

                    REINA
        (Said very quickly)
Oh God, yes.

                    LIVI
Okay. I wake up, he's curled around me. And I'm really just relaxed,
and warm. I haven't used my electric blanket the two months he's been
here. I hardly want to leave but my stomach is making noises and I'm
afraid I'll wake him.

                    REINA
Uh-huh!

                    LIVI
So I slip away silently and into the kitchen. In the fridge, I find this
breakfast sandwich. It has my name on it.

                    REINA
Oh!

                    LIVI
It's an egg freetata or frittata, not sure how he pronounces it, but I get
the ketchup, and as I lift the top piece of bread off to add it. There *it* is.
So beautiful. Perfect really. See, he's written in cap-ers, or capers, I
don't know, but they're little and green and they spell "Marry Me."

                    REINA
"Marry Me."

                    LIVI

Anyway, so then he comes paddling out in his slippers, his cheeks all rosy. And he looks so adorable. And there was really nothing left to say but... "Yes."
> (Beat)

Thanks for helping me get him moved in, Rey.
> (Calling out door)

Pax, you sure you're okay, honey?

PAX

> (offstage)

I'm just fine!

LIVI

Oh no. It's almost—. Have we kept you too long? Reina, if you have to go, get back to Barry and Adam...

REINA

No, Barry's working late and Adam's at soccer practice so—

> (Pax enters, loaded down with boxes, and places them with the others)

LIVI

Pax you should've let me help.

PAX

I'm fine, I'm fine.

REINA

What do you want to do with all these? Should we put them in—

PAX

Not yet. Let's just...
> (Catching his breath)

Let's just rest a second.
> (Pax sits)

REINA

Hey, how about a snack, while we rest? My treat. I told Barry to put some money in my purse this morning so...let's see...hmmm...*three dollars*...

LIVI

That's okay, Rey—

REINA

No, let's see. Well, the only other thing I have is one of Barry's checks but...I have to use this for groceries later...

                         PAX
Really, you're helping us, we'll treat—

                         REINA
Oh, now I feel so—

                         .LIVI
Don't. I'll go make a call. Pizza okay?

                         PAX
Pizza?

                         REINA
(simultaneous to: Pizza?) Fine by me.

        (Livi exits)

                         PAX
Why only one check?

                         REINA
Pardon?

                         PAX
Why not the whole book?

                         REINA
Oh, Barry likes to make sure we save and I think he's afraid if I had the
whole book—

                         PAX
Ah.

                         REINA
It's *okay.* He's just being careful, is all. It's not like he's... I mean he's
generous to me. Last spring he paid to have some improvements done
to the kitchen. Of course, then he joked, he said "now you can spend
more time in there making my meals" but... but it was really done out of
a...well, he likes to kid....
        (beat)
So. Livi tells me you want to start your own restaurant?

                         PAX
Yes. It's going to be like nothing you've ever seen. It'll be called "The
Garden." Idyllic outdoor setting. Vines. Flowers. *Fruit* trees. Fresh
vegetables *growing*. A man-made stream. Runs outside. Runs *inside*.
And in it. Swimming. Are Copper River salmon. And they're *on* the
menu.
        (Livi enters)

REINA

It sounds...creative.

PAX

No market for it here, though. But in the City of Stars—

REINA

City of Stars...

LIVI

He means L.A.

PAX

In the City of Stars it could be the next big thing. And while I'm cooking, Livi could be auditioning—

LIVI

He likes to fantasize about moving to Hollywood and making it—

PAX

(over "making it") Livi, I need you to believe in this. (To Reina:) I'm not fantasizing.   Has she told you, one of the men at the home, Mr. Fine, his son is a talent scout—

LIVI

Is rumored to be—

PAX

You've gotta work those connections, Liv. That's the way it works in the City of Stars—

REINA

City of Stars. Where have I heard that...wait! Livi, is this today's mail?

LIVI

Yeah?

REINA

I just read this incredible thing about the City of Stars...not LA but...where was it....oh. Here. The community college mailer—. Ah. I was close. The course is called *Cities Among the Stars.* I just found this so fascinating. Listen to this: "Paradise. Impossible on earth. But is it possible in space? Professor R. Stern, M.A., contends that in the isolation of space, unique social experiments could result in utopian success stories...in this six week course—"

PAX

Are you going to take this course?

                    REINA
Oh, no. I wouldn't do that.

                    PAX
But you're so interested.

                    REINA
No, I just thought it was a nice conversation starter, um...I mean...look,
it starts this afternoon.

                    PAX
But clearly you have a spark for this.

                    REINA
You think?

                    PAX
Definitely.

                    REINA
I don't know, I haven't asked Barry, and besides I'd have to register
today...before five...and...I don't even have any money on me...

                    PAX
What about that check?

                    LIVI
Pax, that's for her groceries.

        (Reina eyes the check in her hand)

                    PAX
But she has a *spark*. You don't think Barry would say yes?

SCENE 5:

(Barry and Reina's bedroom)

(In blackness we hear sounds of grunting, exertion, and the following
dialogue)

                    BARRY
YES! YES! YES! YES! Now you scream "yes" too. You scream "yes"!

                    REINA
Okay. Please. We're done.

                                BARRY
I will make you come! I will make you come!

                                REINA
I have to finish my homework.

                                BARRY
Five more minutes!

                                REINA
That's *it,* Barry. I'm turning on the light.

          (Reina claps twice. The lights come on)

          (Barry and Reina are in bed, under the covers, Reina is wearing
          a t-shirt and is putting on some boxers)

                                BARRY
          (Glancing at his wrist watch)
Guess I can catch the tail end of Magnum P.I.
          (Reina heads for the door)
You're not running off to do that before you finish folding the laundry,
though, right?

                                REINA
Barry!

                                BARRY
You want me to go to work, my clothes all *crumpled* tomorrow?

          (Reluctantly, Reina begins folding. She folds absently and thus
          badly with one hand, while looking over some notes. Barry
          notices, lets a long breath out, but says nothing. He grabs the
          remote off the bedside table and flips on the TV. After a
          moment).

                                BARRY
Don't see what the big deal is. It's a life-long learning class. Not like it
matters what grade you get.

                                REINA
(over "you get") It's broadening me.

          (A long pause, during which he watches TV and she folds
          poorly).

                                REINA
Can't you understand? What I'm learning – it's *important* – to, like, all
mankind.

——

                              BARRY
"Cities in Space."

                              REINA
It's *"Cities Among the Stars."*

                              BARRY
Sounds like a fruity class to me.

                              REINA
It's an incredible class. My teacher is brilliant.

                              BARRY
(over "my teacher is brilliant") It's community college!

                              REINA
Robert says—

                              BARRY
Can I watch this?

                              REINA
Robert says cities among the stars are mankind's best chance at survival
—

                              BARRY
Robert? One class and you're on a first name basis with the guy?

                              REINA
He says we're the first species on the planet smart enough to escape
extinction, but we probably aren't *mature* enough to use our brains to do
it.

                              BARRY
Can you at least *hang* my collared shirts?

        (She begins hanging his shirts. Several are already haphazardly
        folded. She picks those up and will hang them as well during the
        following).

                              REINA
He says that we only have limited resources to do it though, and that
we're using them up on stupid things instead. Like weapons of mass
destruction—

                              BARRY
(over "destruction...") Okay, Reina. I'm trying to *relax.* Could you get
me some pretzels?

(Barry continues watching the TV)

REINA

See, you're part of the *problem*. All you wanna do is sit on your ass and watch TV, these stupid *reruns*, and eat pretzels.

BARRY

And a Coke. Could you see if we have a Coke in the 'fridge?

REINA

Robert gave us an assignment, that we should think about how we could each *help* the *cause*. And I thought about it and I've decided I would like to become an astronaut.

BARRY

An astronaut?

REINA

Robert thinks it's a good idea.

BARRY

Sounds like a fruity quack to me.

REINA

(over "to me") He thinks I should go for it. I downloaded the application off the NASA website and everything.

> (Barry puts the TV on "mute," looks at her for a second, shakes his head in disbelief, and goes back to staring at the TV. He turns the volume, and takes a big breath in and out, trying to relax. Reina watches Barry)

SCENE 6:

(Livi and Pax's apartment)

(Livi enters, wearing scrubs, holding a tiara. Pax holds a large salad bowl at crotch level, which he stirs with a wooden spoon. He appears to be naked).

PAX

Hi honey. How was work? What are you doing with a tiara?

LIVI

What are you doing in boxers?

PAX

I've decided I cook better in boxers.

                    LIVI
Why?

                    PAX
I believe I asked you about the *tiara* first.

                    LIVI
It's freezing, it's like five degrees in here.

                    PAX
The *tiara.*

                    LIVI
Mr. Fine has been calling me "princess" all week. He likes to joke.

                    PAX
Okay...?

                    LIVI
He keeps joking "where is your crown, where is your crown?" So today,
I figure, why not *wear* one for him.

                    PAX
Where'd you get it?

                    LIVI
Oh, I had it.

                    PAX
From?

                    LIVI
It's a stupid story....

                    PAX
You got it for being stupid?

                    LIVI
Funny. I got it for being pretty.

                    PAX
You are pretty.

                    LIVI

I was fourteen. For some reason, my guidance counselor took an interest in me. Who knows *what* she saw in me – wearing Barry's hand-me-down rugby shirts... But she entered me in a local beauty pageant. Bought me a nice dress, and some makeup and everything. Got me all dolled up....
>   (Beat)
It's a silly story.

                              PAX

Go on.

                              LIVI

Well, the night of the pageant came – and she tried to get my dad there. But of course he wouldn't... And then...I won. *I* won. I couldn't *believe* it. And they gave me this tiara. I remember getting home and being so proud – and there was Dad, sitting on his Lazy-Boy, watching something funny on TV, 'cause he was laughing – just really in a good mood. Well, I just waited, patiently, until the commercial. Then I walked up to him, tapped him on the shoulder, ever so lightly, and showed him my tiara – my *crown.* And this part, I'll never forget, he actually smiled at me – he touched my face – and he said "Are you my Miss America? Are you my little Miss Universe?" At that moment, I *had* his attention. He was looking right at me. And I remember, thinking it was really weird, because I'd never noticed how blue his eyes were before.

                              PAX

Put it on.

                              LIVI

What?

                              PAX

Model it for me. Please.
>   (She does)
Beautiful.

                              LIVI

You think?

                              PAX

Absolutely. Check yourself out in the mirror.

>   (He brings the mirror to her)

                              LIVI

Mr. Fine said I looked "stunning."

                              PAX

You do.

28

                              LIVI

Oh, come on. In scrubs?

                              PAX

Even in scrubs, Livi.

                              LIVI

Anyway, he asked me...and it was a little strange, but, he asked me if
I'd...show him a little leg.

                              PAX

Oh jeez. Did you?

                              LIVI

You know. We take for granted. As adults. These little adult
kindnesses we get. Adult flirtations, intimacies, moments of respect.
They're so *deprived*. Most of the Care Aids patronize them – like they're
children.

                              PAX

So you did? You showed some –

                              LIVI

Only for a second.

                              PAX

Best second of his day.

                              LIVI

For our residents. Attention. It's like. Manna in the desert for them.

                              PAX

Listen. You ever think of...auditioning for him?

                              LIVI

What?

                              PAX

I mean, doing a monologue or something – something so he'd see your
talent –

                              LIVI

Why?

                              PAX

I mean, if his son's a talent scout—

                              LIVI

No one knows that for sure.

                    PAX
Just an idea. Listen, I want you to try this salad.

                    LIVI
That you made in boxers?

                    PAX
It *helps* the salad.

                    LIVI
Cooking in boxers helps the salad?

                    PAX
I think it does. Cooking all dressed up is the socially normal thing to do.
An artist exists beyond what is socially normal.

                    LIVI
Ah yes, my food *artiste*. You're adorable.

                    PAX
When I'm cooking, this feels more comfortable, more primal, more
animalistic.

                    LIVI
The salad does look artful. Are those strawberries? In a dinner salad?

                    PAX
Yes! For color. It's *art* meant to be devoured. It's like Tibetan sand
painting.

                    LIVI
They eat sand in Tibet?

                    PAX
No, no, this salad is *like* Tibetan sand painting. In Tibet the artist crafts
intricate images painstakingly, using millions of vegetable-dyed grains.
It takes a very long time. Upon completion, all of its manifest beauty is
appreciated for but a single moment, before it's swept up, poured into
an urn. Yes, after all of that struggle for creation, there is only one
moment of perception. One moment of beauty before all is returned to
formless dust.
         (Pax hands Livi a bowl)
No sooner is the salad made. Tasted. It is gone.

         (Pax sits by Livi, watching her intently).

                    LIVI

30

This is really very pretty.

                              PAX
Try it. Tell me if you think people would pay to eat this.

          (Livi gets up, moving to the kitchen)

                              LIVI
Do we have any Thousand Island left?

                              PAX
There's already dressing on it.

                              LIVI
A little more can't hurt.
          (Livi exits, Pax follows to the exit but stops, calling after her)

                              PAX
But it will. The dressing on there is delicate. It's cilantro lime. It brings
out the natural flavor of the vegetables.

                              LIVI
          (offstage)
I'm sure it does! Where's the bottle? You didn't hide it, did you?

                              PAX
Must you put ketchup on everything?

                              LIVI
It's not ketchup. It's Thousand Island.
          (She enters with Thousand Island dressing and approaches the
          salad)

                              PAX
Would you smack a coat of house paint on a Picasso? I mean. I
wonder. You think Olga Koklova smacked globs of sheer crap onto his
finished canvases?

                              LIVI
Olga Kla-who?

                              PAX
Picasso's first wife. I mean, you think *Guernica* would have been the
same work of genius if he'd let her cover it in Thousand Island?!

                              LIVI
Why would you put salad dressing on a painting?

                              PAX

Why are you taking everything so literally?!

                    LIVI
Can you be patient with me?

                    PAX
Can I be—

                    LIVI
Before I met you...I mean, I've never seen a salad with strawberries in it before...what's that white stuff?

                    PAX
Gorgonzola.

                    LIVI
What's that?

                    PAX
It's a cheese. Look, this is a new experience, Livi. I understand that, but...

                    LIVI
So just...let me use my dressing. Just for now, huh?
        (She waits for a moment, then puts Thousand Island dressing on
        the salad, slapping the back of the bottle and slowly eats).
This isn't bad. I bet they will like it when you open your restaurant.

                    PAX
Yeah.

                    LIVI
No, really. It's a very creative salad.

                    PAX
Thanks.

                    LIVI
So...have you thought about what you're going to do in the meantime?

                    PAX
In the meantime?

                    LIVI
While you're trying to get your restaurant started. You know. A job?

                    PAX
Oh, I tried a little this week. They're scared to take a risk. Soon as I say "self-trained chef" they just stop listening.

LIVI
Well. I was talking to Barry today. He's...one of his friends runs the
Steak 'n Shake...

PAX
You want me to take a job at a Steak 'n Shake? No. No way – never.

SCENE 7:

(Barry and Reina's bedroom)

(Reina lies on the bed, looking over some notes and writing. Barry
enters, and begins undressing down to his boxers during the following)

BARRY
Great day today. I'm tellin' ya, havin' those apple pies in the store – my
best idea. Sit the customer down. Give 'em a slice. *A' la mode.* Get
'em real relaxed. Talk computers, talk home entertainment... I moved
over twenty thousand in merchandise. *Today.* I'm on *fire*, Reina. I
keep going like this, we'll have enough for that swimming pool; *in-
ground.*
        (beat)
Adam home?

REINA
Out with friends.

(Barry gets into bed, and starts rubbing Reina's leg)

BARRY
You wanna *celebrate*?

REINA
What?

BARRY
My *sales*!

REINA
I'm concentrating, Barry.

BARRY
        (Moving his hand up her stomach)
More of that Astronaut crap.

REINA
It's not crap.

                    BARRY
        (Puts his hand on her breast)
C'mon...
        (Kissing her neck)
Astronauts have to know stuff. Science.

                    REINA
I took chemistry in college.

                    BARRY
        (Starts to undo her pants)
(over "in college") Astronauts are real smart. Got good grades in
college. They *finished.*

                    REINA
        (She zips her pants back up)
It was circumstances. I had Adam, I—

                    BARRY
You've got no *qualifications.*

                    REINA
I've got a spark.

        (Notices his video camera)

                    BARRY
You got my video camera out.

                    REINA
I'm making a video.

                    BARRY
        (Looking toward the camera as he moves in on her)
Is it on?

                    REINA
        (Pushing him away)
To send to *NASA.* A video *essay.*   Don't bother me.

                    BARRY
You're my wife. Who else should I bother? Fine. Guess I can catch the
tail end of Magnum P.I.
        (Barry reaches for the remote, Reina gets back into bed,
        blocking his way)

                    REINA

So I don't have all those qualifications astronauts are supposed to have.
So what? Should I just not even try? I mean, do I want to end up on
my *deathbed* regretting I never even *tried*?

                    BARRY
          (Touching her again)
Forget about it, honey.

                    REINA
No. I mean. Forget credentials. Right? I have something more
important.

                    BARRY
A great ass. Come here.
          (Pulls her toward him)

                    REINA
I have vision. I *see* the importance of what NASA is doing. I want to be
part of it. To contribute. To do something meaningful.
          (Barry pulls her to him)
Barry, would you *PLEASE* stop being such a *SNAKE*.

          (Barry leans back, hurt. Pause)

                    BARRY
I *miss* you.

SCENE 8:

(Livi and Pax's apartment)

(Livi enters).

                    LIVI
Pax?! Honey!? Are you home?

                    PAX
          (offstage)
In the kitchen!

                    LIVI
How was your first day at Steak 'n Shake?

                    PAX
          (offstage)
Culinary Purgatory! The food they have me cooking is *disgusting*. It's
Philistine cuisine!

(Pax enters, carrying two large bowls. As before, he is dressed
    in only boxers).
But at least I can come home and cook wonderful feasts for my love.

                         LIVI
What is it?

                         PAX
Could you grab the wine?

                         LIVI
Sure. Looks pretty as always.
    (She exits to kitchen, Pax follows to kitchen entrance, staying
    onstage)

                         PAX
On the bottom is a bed of jasmine risotto in a coconut milk infusion. On
top is free-range chicken. Sliced paper thin and prepped in a lemon-
cilantro marinade.
    (Livi enters with wine and ketchup, sits at table)
I've thrown some red belle pepper in – for color. And some caramelized
sweet onions. They go *amazing* with the chicken, which goes *amazing*
with the coconut...
    (Pax follows after, placing both bowls on the table)
It's a gestalt of flavor.
    (Livi dumps ketchup all over hers, slapping the back of the
    bottle. Pax rubs his head, frustrated)

                         LIVI
What?

                         PAX
Nothing.

                         LIVI
Relax. Sit down. Have some wine.
    (He sits, but makes no move to eat or drink).
What?

                         PAX
Nothing.

                         LIVI
You sure?

        (Pause)

                         PAX
So...you audition for Mr. Fine today?

                         LIVI
Is that what you were whispering last night?

                         PAX
What are you talking about?

                         LIVI
I was drifting off and I heard this whisper: "Audition for Mr. Fine.
Audition for Mr. Fine."

                         PAX
You must have dreamt it.

                         LIVI
Pax. Sometimes I feel like...you're holding things back. Not
saying...what you're thinking? Or in this case, *doing*?

                         PAX
C'mon.

                         LIVI
No, really. I think a relationship. *Any* relationship has to be built on a
foundation of total honesty...

                         PAX
Yeah...

                         LIVI
So if you're holding anything back...keeping any deep, dark little secrets
from me...

                         PAX
Fine. Yes. I whispered "Audition for Mr. Fine" in your ear last night.

                         LIVI
That's screwed up.

                         PAX
I was just trying to help you dream—

                         LIVI
Well it worked.

                         PAX
It did?

                         LIVI
I made an ass out of myself today.

                              PAX
You auditioned for him?

                              LIVI
I did a monologue, yes.

                              PAX
Fantastic? How did it go?

                              LIVI
I can't believe you *toyed* with my subconscious – and without *asking*.
Do you have any other dark little secrets I should know about?

                              PAX
No.
        (Beat)
Well. Maybe one.

                              LIVI
Maybe one?

                              PAX
How did your audition go?

                              LIVI
You can't just say "maybe one" and continue to ask about my audition.

                              PAX
How did it go?

                              LIVI
I did a monologue at an old folks home – that's hardly an audition.
What's the secret?

                              PAX
What happened?

                              LIVI
Mr. Fine got all excited and said I'd have to show his son...

                              PAX
The talent scout!

                              LIVI
No one knows if he really is a talent scout. That's just what Mr. Fine
says. Tell me your secret!

                              PAX

This could be great. You never know.

                              LIVI
Yeah well...

                              PAX
Weirder things have happened. This could be your big *break.*

                              LIVI
Pax. I'm happy. *Where* I *am.* I made an intentional *decision.*

                              PAX
Not to pursue your dream.

                              LIVI
I'm a Care Aid.

                              PAX
And you hate it.

                              LIVI
I don't. It's a rewarding life.

                              PAX
Do you want it to be the *rest* of your life?
      (Beat)

                              LIVI
I don't want to talk about this. I want to talk about your secret.

                              PAX
No, you *have* something. The way our entire school *stopped.* To take
notice.

                              LIVI
(over "to take notice") What did they know? It was *high school.* I was a
child.

                              PAX
You got into Julliard!

                              LIVI
That was a fluke—

                              PAX
Was *The Sound of Music* a fluke? Afterwards there wasn't a single
person who didn't know your name. Have you forgotten the way people
responded? Is it even possible you forget something like that?

LIVI

What's the point in remembering?

PAX

Remember for me.

LIVI

Tell me your secret.

PAX

Remember, and I'll tell you.

LIVI

Tell me and I'll remember.
(Pause)

PAX

You know...my brother, Bret...

LIVI

Yeah...?

PAX

He doesn't exist. I'm an only child.

LIVI

You made him up?

PAX

I *had* to. You know how Barry and his buddies were always picking on Russ Weinberg in high school... I was afraid I was going to be next so I...I *invented* Bret. Ya know. Big brother Bret, who was in the Marines – who'd kick their ass if they messed with me...

LIVI

You're an only child?

PAX

Yes. Now tell me. I want to know what you remember.

LIVI

No.

PAX

You promised.

LIVI

I remember how everyone got quiet, okay?
(Beat)

Quiet...and still. Like they were all connected to me. All a part of me.
Even Dad and Barry – I looked out, even they were...seeing me. I
mean, *really* seeing me. And at the end of the show, when I stepped
forward to take my bow the applause was—was—

                              PAX
It was deafening, Livi. In a little high school auditorium. It was
deafening and you don't think—

                              LIVI
Dad and Barry were applauding with the rest of them. They had these
big smiles on their face. Afterwards Dad took us out to dinner. And I
was thinking, this is it, ya know.

                              PAX
Totally.

                              LIVI
He's finally seen what they all see.

                              PAX
Yes.

                              LIVI
We sit down. The first words out of his mouth are "Sure, you were OK,
but I'm not really sure you've got the movie star look. Take Annette
Benning – she's real tall, isn't she, Barry?" "Oh yeah, Liv," Barry says,
"movie stars are real tall." So I'm like, "What about Marilyn Monroe?
She was short." And Dad just looks at Barry and says "Now she thinks
she's Marilyn Monroe." And they just laugh and laugh.

                              PAX
Livi....

                              LIVI
Dad wanted me to come work at the Techno-Hut. He didn't want me to
leave.

                              PAX
Are you truly happy having stayed?

                              LIVI
Yes. No. I don't know. I live a good life here.

                              PAX
I'm not happy here. I can't work at the Steak'n Shake forever.

                              LIVI
I know.

PAX

I was thinking maybe tomorrow, after my shift, I could go to the bank, see about a loan for my restaurant, for "The Garden."

LIVI

That'd be good.

PAX

Yes, but I don't want to open it here, Liv. I want to open it out there, in the City of Stars. Can you imagine it? You and I in the City of Stars – Stars everywhere. Me, feeding them, you rubbing elbows with them...
        (beat)
But we can't do it unless you believe.

SCENE 9:

(Grocery store)

(Reina enters, pushing on a shopping cart)

REINA

Come on, Barr—stop dawdling.

BARRY

        (off)
I'm coming, I'm coming.
        (Barry enters)

REINA

Barry, the post office closes in twenty minutes. If my application package isn't post-marked today—

BARRY

I try to do a nice thing. Keep you company on your *chores*—

REINA

You're only here to make sure I don't use your check on another class.

BARRY

Not true. I'm just keeping you company, being a dutiful husband—
        (He kisses her on the cheek)
—and you're rushing me.

REINA

I wouldn't have to rush you if we had taken the route I wanted and swung by the post office on the way here.

                    BARRY

Who stopped you?

                    REINA

You did.

                    BARRY

Nah.

                    REINA

Yes! You *insisted* we drive the other way so we could stop at *Steak 'n Shake* first.

                    BARRY

Well, didn't you enjoy the *Steak 'n Shake*?

                    REINA

I don't think you understand how important this package is.

                    BARRY

Yeah, yeah. I understand. I understand.

                    REINA

Do you understand the "eggs in one basket" theory?

                    BARRY

What?

                    REINA

Robert says our planet is like an egg carton and we're like the eggs in it—

                    BARRY

What the fuck?

                    REINA

(continuous) And any number of things could come along and shatter them all. So why are we keeping them all in one basket? I mean why aren't we working on ways to take a few eggs out of the one basket and put them in other baskets, say in space, for safe keeping?

                    BARRY

I'm sure we are working on ways to do that, Rey.

                    REINA

No, we're not. That's what's amazing. That's why I have to join NASA, become an astronaut, and push for Robert's cause.

                    BARRY

Yeah, okay, okay. Could we not talk about this? People are uh...

                              REINA
(over "People are uh") Do you know the national budget is four hundred
billion for military this year, we're not even spending a tenth of that on
space technologies? We're working on better ways to kill, not better
ways to live.

                              BARRY
Better ways to kill *are* ways to live. I don't want to discuss this here.

                              REINA
You never want to discuss this.

                              BARRY
It's embarrassing!
          (beat)
Oh, shit. Apple pie. I forgot apple pie.

                              REINA
Don't you dare.

                              BARRY
I'll be right back.

                              REINA
That's all the way at the other end of the store. We don't have time.

                              BARRY
I need an apple pie for the Techno-Hut, Rey.

                              REINA
I need to mail this package.

                              BARRY
Look, Rey. It'll take me five minutes. I'm going.

                              REINA
Give me the car keys.

                              BARRY
I'll meet you at the checkout line.

                              REINA
Barry!
          (Barry exits. Reina looks after him)
Fine, I'll *walk* there if I have to! I'll *walk* there!
          (She exits, pushing her cart off)

___

44

(In a different part of the grocery store, Pax, holds a shopping basket and reads a paper. Barry enters, with an apple pie and glides it in between Pax and his paper).

BARRY

Apple Pie.   Tempting, huh?

PAX

Oh. Barry.

BARRY

You want this?
        (Pax shakes his head "no")
Where's Livi?

PAX

At home.

BARRY

So you're the *woman* today, eh?

PAX

We share responsibilities—

BARRY

The *little lady.*
        (Barry laughs, slapping Pax on the ass)
You sure you don't want this? It's good stuff. Here ya go. The forbidden fruit pie.

PAX

Actually, I've already got more than I intended....
        (Barry places the pie in Pax's basket)

BARRY

So Reina tells me you're starting your own restaurant?   You're calling it "The Plantation" or something?

PAX

"The Garden."

BARRY

What kinda place is that? Vegetarian?

PAX

It won't be strictly vegetarian, no.

BARRY

Huh. Sounds great.

                    PAX

What?

                    BARRY

Yeah. I'm jazzed, man. Tell me more.

                    PAX

Oh. Okay. Um. I'm going for something entirely new. A cuisine that
breaks into uncharted territories of taste.

                    BARRY

Nice. Nice. Fuck, yeah.

                    PAX

Wish the bank thought that.

                    BARRY

Wouldn't give you a loan, huh?

                    PAX

They said I needed collateral, *home equity,* or some shit.

                    BARRY

Shit. Hey, listen. I'd love to hear more about this.

                    PAX

You would?

                    BARRY

Sure, I mean, I've got home equity and... Hey is your face okay?

                    PAX

My face?

                    BARRY

Looks a bit hacked up. How 'bout you come down to the Techno-Hut?
We'll talk more about your restaurant and we can get you an electric
razor—

                    PAX

My razor's fine.

                    BARRY

And you've got a few nose hairs hanging out there. Yeah.   We've got a
whole male grooming kit. Come down to the Hut, we'll...talk.
          (Barry exits. Pax goes back to the paper. After a moment, he
          drops the basket, still staring at the paper).

___

PAX

Oh my God.

SCENE 10:

(Livi and Pax's apartment)

PAX

There I was, I'd chopped the vegetables and I was stirring the pot. Suddenly, I felt uncertain – like gripped with panic. I wasn't sure if there was water in the pot, and the pot started to look like a deep, dark well – I wasn't sure if it wasn't actually empty – if the water wasn't just illusion, a fabrication of my mind. I had this feeling like I was falling down into this empty well. And, I was doing what you would do, if the well were full with water, and you weren't actually falling, but sinking. You would doggie paddle like mad to reach the top. But you just keep falling, because it's just air. And then there's that moment...you realize...there's no water...so you might as well stop paddling and just give in, just let yourself fall.
        (beat)
I started making soup but then I...gave in. I don't know what we're going to do about dinner tonight.

LIVI

Pax...what's wrong?

PAX

It's in the paper.

LIVI

"Flight controllers rejoice at the successful landing of the Rover Spirit on mars." That's what you're—that's good right, that's progress for mankind, hope—it shouldn't make you feel—

PAX

Look on the other side.

LIVI

"Woman found dead in Neiman Marcus display window."

PAX

She loved Neiman Marcus.

LIVI

Who?

PAX

My grandmother.

                              LIVI
Oh, Pax...

                              PAX
She had a stroke. Sometimes they come in waves, the first wave must
have confused her, who knows why, but she wandered into one of the
displays. A window shopper and her little daughter were the first to see
her, lying there, among the latest fashions...

                              LIVI
That's horrible.

                              PAX
My parents have known since yesterday. They neglected to tell me.
This is how I find out. Mom said "we've just been non-stop the last few
days." Evidently, planning some party for one of Dad's business
partners was more important than...

                              LIVI
God.

                              PAX
Am I silly for wanting to do this so intensely?

                              LIVI
What?

                              PAX
Cook.

                              LIVI
No, you've got so much creativity—

                              PAX
So did she. We never even knew, but so did she. See, I went to her
place today. Just to feel...near her. You know. The smell of mothballs.

                              LIVI
They're comforting.

                              PAX
Familiar. I go through her closet, right? Just looking at all her things.
And I find, in the back – this old bureau. Never even knew it was there.
And in it, in the bottom drawer are all these old comic strips. Hand
drawn. Signed with her initials...

                              LIVI
She drew comics—?

———

                                    PAX
(over "drew comics") We never even *knew.* She used to call Charles
Schultz a "glorified hack" and occasionally she'd randomly bellow "damn
that Schultz." We never understood. You could see the years of effort.
There had to be a hundred finished comic strips there, easy. One
hundred pieces of my grandma's life, one hundred chances she must
have never cashed in – one hundred of her dreams, sitting, mildewed in
the bottom of a drawer...
        (beat)
You know Grandpa didn't even *like* the comics, Livi. He wouldn't buy the
Sunday paper *on principle.* But what if he *had,* Livi? If he'd believed in
her, pushed her...what could she have been?
        (beat)
Livi, I need you to...*say* something.

                                    LIVI
I auditioned for Mr. Fine's son today.

                                    PAX
What?

                                    LIVI
He finally came to visit today and I...I took my shot.

                                    PAX
So he really is a—

                                    LIVI
He works for William Morris.

                                    PAX
Who is?

                                    LIVI
Catherine Zeta-Jones is with them—

                                    PAX
A talent agency.

                                    LIVI
The Talent Agency.   He thinks I'd be good in movies. He said I have...a
unique look.

                                    PAX
I've always thought that.

                                    LIVI
He said, if I ever come out to L.A....he could really *do* something for me.

                    PAX
Livi. Livi. Livi!

                    LIVI
What?!

                    PAX
A—a star-maker has descended from the City of Stars to grant you a
chance!

                    LIVI
I know.

                    PAX
This can't just be coincidence – it's, it's a divine sign!

                    LIVI
What's a divine sign?

                    PAX
A chance landed in my lap today, too. For "The Garden."

                    LIVI
Really?!

                    PAX
The gods are with us today, they are speaking to us, and they are
speaking through Barry!

                    LIVI
Barry?

                    PAX
He has home equity. It's the collateral I need to get a start-up loan.

                    LIVI
Pax, Barry won't—

                    PAX
I ran into him this morning. At the grocery store. I told him about "The
Garden." He seemed interested.

                    LIVI
Was he trying to sell you something?

                    PAX
Hope can come in the strangest forms, Livi.

———

                              LIVI
I don't know—

                              PAX
We'll invite him and Reina to dinner here tomorrow night. Barry can try
my food, so he feels secure about backing me, and then we can be—we
will be on our way to the City of Stars – the City of Stars! Oh! I've got
to get cooking. Livi, thank you! Yet again there are meats to marinate,
veggies to julienne, and sauces to simmer! And it's all thanks to you!

SCENE 11:

(Barry and Reina's Bedroom)

(Barry sits on the bed watching TV. Reina enters.   Barry turns off the
TV)

                              REINA
Adam's sitter is here.

                              BARRY
Good.

                              REINA
They're both glued to his X-Box.

                              BARRY
Uh-huh. Come here.
          (He pats the empty space on the bed)

                              REINA
Why aren't you dressed? We have to be at Pax and Livi's in half an
hour.

                              BARRY
We got time. Only takes five minutes to drive over there. Sit.

                              REINA
Fine.
          (Reina sits beside him on the bed)
What?

                              BARRY
I wanna try something.
          (Barry kisses up her neck and nibbles on her ear)

                              REINA
What are you doing?

BARRY

You like that?

REINA

It's OK.

BARRY

Read about that in *Man Magazine*. "How to please your woman." Is it *pleasing* you?

REINA

Well...

BARRY

It's supposed to feel *great* with *this*.
          (Barry sucks right between the base of her neck and shoulder)

REINA

Oh, *Barry.*

BARRY

Nice, huh?

REINA

Yeah.
          (They begin making out, getting more and more intense. Reina breaks off)

BARRY

What are you—

REINA

My diaphragm—

BARRY

Forget about that.
          (He pulls her to him, and between kisses, he says)
I've been thinking, Adam's getting *older* now. In like, four years he's gonna be a *teenager*. Maybe it's time we start thinking of having another –
          (Reina is up, out of bed, fast)
What? What did I say?

REINA

I want to be an astronaut.

BARRY

So?

                    REINA
Whoever heard of a pregnant astronaut?

                    BARRY
Well I've heard of pregnant astronauts—

                    REINA
Barry, you're trying to—

                    BARRY
I'm not trying to anything!

                    REINA
Robert would say you're being irresponsible.

                    BARRY
For wanting to have a happy family with the woman I love?

                    REINA
For wanting to overpopulate the planet.

                    BARRY
I just want to—

                    REINA
If we don't make space habitable in the next few generations, overpopulation will be a huge problem.

                    BARRY
Fine. Use a diaphragm.

                    REINA
Forget it.

                    BARRY
Come back to bed.

                    REINA
We have to leave soon, anyway. Get dressed.

                    BARRY
We *have* to?

                    REINA
Yes. I *promised* your sister.

                    BARRY
Come here.

REINA

I'll be downstairs.
          (Reina exits)

SCENE 12:

(Livi and Pax's Apartment)

(Pax enters in a tuxedo, placing a tablecloth over the table, followed by cloth napkins, silverware, and fine china. Livi enters from work, in scrubs)

LIVI

Sorry, I'm late. Traffic was—

PAX

Quick. Put on something nice. Barry will be here any moment.

LIVI

You're *sweating.*

PAX

The perspiration of inspiration! Get dressed!

LIVI

You look feverish.

PAX

I'm feverish with excitement.

LIVI
          (putting her hand to his forehead)
No, just plain *feverish.* You should lie down.
          (moving to the phone)
I'll call Barry and cancel.

PAX
          (running to beat her to the phone)
No! Don't touch the phone!
          (he grabs it)

LIVI

Give it to me.

PAX

I can't.

———

54

                              LIVI
You're in no condition to—

                              PAX
Lightning has struck tonight, Livi. Lightning has struck my mind as if it
were a tree. And my mind has combusted tonight with brilliance.
Hundreds of thoughts like sparks, burning embers, flying and falling like
shooting stars or streaking comets. I'm on *fire.*

                              LIVI
Temperature-wise. Yes.

                              PAX
On fire with inspiration.

                              LIVI
With madness. Give me the phone.

                              PAX
I'm cooking things today, I've never cooked before! That no man has
ever cooked before. A light, chickpea sprout beet salad with chevre –
just came to me like a flash of genius this morning at 3am.

                              LIVI
You were up at—?

                              PAX
(on "at") At 7 AM, suddenly a main course *materialized* before me.   A
vision of roasted capon, in a balsamic marinade, wrapped in banana leaf
and *complemented* by a cantaloupe-pineapple chutney, and spicy
raspberry sauce. And for *dessert*—

                              LIVI
You're *sick.*

                              PAX
With joy! With elation!

                              LIVI
With the flu.

                              PAX
I feel great.

                              LIVI
You're not thinking clearly—

                              PAX

As clear as a cloudless summer day – I'm radiant, like the sun. White hot like a white dwarf, like my white chocolate plum mousse for dessert—

(Livi snatches the phone from him)

LIVI

Got it!

(Livi begins dialing)

PAX

No. Please, Livi. *Please.* Lightning so rarely strikes like *this.* I'm telling you. Today is my *chance.* This is *it.* Let me have it. Let me bask in the glory of this single moment of sublime perfection. *Please.*

LIVI

Barry, hi. Listen, Pax isn't... Oh. You're here.
　　(Doorbell rings)

PAX

I can't do this without you, Livi.

LIVI

Okay. Okay, Pax.

PAX

Okay! I'll get it. Could you—?

LIVI

I'll put on something nice.

(Livi exits. Pax runs to the door, opens it)

PAX

Hello. HELLO! Welcome to our humble abode.

BARRY

(on "abode") ENOUGH ALREADY, REINA! Hi Pax.
　　(Barry walks right by Pax and sits on the couch. Reina follows).

REINA

....you almost *hit* that eighty year old woman.

BARRY

Didn't look eighty to me. At eighty you *don't* run that fast, Reina.

REINA

When you're trying to save your life—

                    BARRY

It's a *need* for *speed.* I'm a man.

                    REINA

How is that an answer? "I'm a man." Like that excuses—

                    BARRY

Well, it's *true.* I am a *man.* You have digital cable, right Pax?

                    PAX

Well actually...

                    BARRY

What say we *men* watch some Magnum P.I. reruns before dinner?
          (Barry reaches for the remote, Pax picks it up before he can
          reach it)
Hey, what's the idea?

                    PAX

Actually, um, the idea is dinner will be served in a few minutes.

                    REINA

Enough with the Magnum P.I. Always with the Magnum PI. No one else
likes that show, Barry.

                    BARRY

Hey, that show lasted 8 years. If no one liked it would it have lasted 8
years?

          (Barry looks at Pax in his tuxedo)

What's with the penguin suit?

          (Pax pulls out a chair for Barry. Livi enters dressed nicely)

                    PAX

Have a seat and we'll begin.

                    BARRY

Hey, Livi. What's with the penguin suit?

                    REINA

Leave it alone, Barry.

                    BARRY

I will *not* leave it alone. I want to know WHAT IS WITH THE
GODDAMNED PENGUIN SUIT!!??

(beat. Pax, wavering, is losing balance, as he helps to set the
table, he collapses)

                              LIVI
Pax, are you okay, honey?

                              BARRY
What's *wrong* with him?

                              PAX
          (Getting up)
I'll be fine. Just a little dizzy. The dinner *must* go on!
          (He walks a step and collapses)

                              LIVI
Pax!

                              REINA
He alright?

                              BARRY
WHAT'S GOING ON!?

                              PAX
Nothing. Nothing. Just lost my balance for a second. We'll start dinner
in just a moment.
          (to Livi)
Maybe I'll just lay down. For a second. Serve... Serve the salad. I'll be
right out.
          (Pax exits)

                              BARRY
What'd he say? Where's he going? Is he going *out* somewhere? Is
there a wedding?

                              LIVI
Pax would like us to start without him.

                              BARRY
Where'd he *go*?

                              LIVI
To rest for a moment, Barry.

                              BARRY
He not *feel* good?

                              LIVI
He's a bit under the weather.

                                BARRY
So what are we *doing* here?

                                LIVI
Pax wants this. Come on. Have a seat.

                                BARRY
Maybe we should just...

                                LIVI
Come *on*, Barry.

                                BARRY
Okay, alright.
        (Barry gets up)
Reina. (meaning, "follow me")

                                REINA
Don't bark at me.

        (They all sit at the table)

                                BARRY
So. How's *life*?

                                LIVI
Fine.

                                BARRY
Work?

                                LIVI
Good.

                                BARRY
That job is crap, Livi.

                                LIVI
Don't start, Barry.

                                BARRY
Okay. Okay.
        (beat)
No place for a girl like you—

                                REINA
Leave her alone, Barry.

                    BARRY
What? What would *you* know about working?

                    LIVI
You're being a *jerk*, Barry.

                    BARRY
Why am I always the jerk?

                    REINA
Good question.

                    BARRY
          (gestures toward the salad)
What is *this*?

                    LIVI
Chickpea beat salad with sprouts and um...chevre.

                    BARRY
Chevre?

                    LIVI
It's goat cheese.

                    REINA
Pax thinks this food has real potential in L.A.

                    BARRY
Hmm.
          (He begins eating)
It's just... I was thinking, Livi—this job of yours—

                    LIVI
It's a good job.

                    BARRY
You've been wiping geriatric ass how many years now?

                    LIVI
This is why I never invite you over.

                    BARRY
How many years?

                    LIVI
Look, I may not be doing it forever.

                    BARRY

Good.

LIVI

I've been thinking of getting back into acting.

BARRY

You're kidding.

REINA

(At same time as "you're kidding") That's wonderful.

LIVI

(To Barry)

No.

BARRY

How about you come work for me?

LIVI

What?

BARRY

You'd be great at the Techno-Hut. You're a woman. All the *men* that come in. You could *move* computers, boy.

LIVI

Why? Because I've got a charming, movie-star presence?

BARRY

Because you're a *woman.*

LIVI

A pretty, charming, talented woman?

BARRY

I don't know, you're my sister.

LIVI

Just *say it*, Barry. I want to hear you say it! I can sell computers because I'm a pretty, charming, talented woman!

BARRY

This is supposed to be a salad? What's in this again?

REINA

Sprouts, chick peas, beets, chevre.

BARRY

(to Reina, genuinely curious)

You *like* it?

                    REINA
        (Takes another taste)
I'm not sure.
        (Beat)
 Maybe this is what they eat out there. In the *City of Stars.*

                    BARRY
        (to Livi)
I don't see what's wrong with the job at the Steak 'n Shake? He's a
cook. It's a good paying job. He gets to *cook.*

                    LIVI
He wants his own restaurant.

                    BARRY
What does he *need* his own restaurant for?

                    LIVI
A sense of autonomy.

                    BARRY
What?

                    REINA
It means independence.

                    BARRY
I know what it means. What does he need that for?

                    LIVI
Look, why don't you just wait? Try all the food. You stand to make
money from this restaurant. Some percent of profits. Until he can pay
the loan back, you'll be considered part owner.

                    REINA
Let's give it a chance, Barry.

                    BARRY
Yeah, *my* money you'll gamble with. Who eats this stuff? Is there a
market?

                    LIVI
Pax thinks there is in L.A...

                    BARRY

I mean. I don't know, Livi. I keep hearing crazy things about the guy from my buddy at the *Steak 'n Shake*. You know he walked in on Pax the other day? While he was cooking. He had his shirt off. Won't keep his shirt on. Evidently he has some problem keeping clothes on when he cooks—

LIVI

It helps him feel free. He's an artist.

BARRY

What *artist*? He's a *cook*! You make sure the meat's brown. You slap some potatoes next to it, and *that's it.*

REINA

Maybe we should just go.

BARRY

(on "go") No, I'll stay. I'll stay.

LIVI

Thank you, Barry.

BARRY

Can I at least watch a little Magnum P.I.? Just until the next course?

LIVI

Fine.
(Barry gets up to watch TV just as Pax enters. Barry sits down begrudgingly).

PAX

And how did you find the salad?

BARRY

We couldn't *find* it. Under all the beets. Ha, ha. Ha, ha.
(Pax looks devastated)
Kidding. I'm kidding, Pax. It was something *different.* Very *interesting.*

REINA

We liked it very much, Pax.

PAX

You didn't *finish.*

BARRY

No, it was fine.

REINA

Saving room, is all.

                          PAX
You're going to *love* the entrée.
          (As Pax places the entrees at each place setting)

                        REINA
Yes, we really are having a lovely time.   Everything is so very new and
novel. And we're really quite impressed with your creativity.

                        BARRY
(muttered) Don't overdo it, Reina.

                          PAX
And here are the garnishes—

                        BARRY
A fruit salad?

                          PAX
A cantaloupe-pineapple chutney. It's got a kick.

                        BARRY
Great. Uh. Thank you.

                          PAX
Sure thing, Barry.

                        BARRY
          (Trying to figure out how to eat it).
  Uh, well...

                          PAX
The banana leaf is for flavor. You can just—
          (Pax leans forward, wretching, despite himself. Pax puts his
          hand to his mouth, Barry leans back, moving his plate out of
          wretching-range).

                         LIVI
Pax? Honey?

                          PAX
Peel it back and—
          (another convulsion)
And enjoy the—
          (another)
Capon.
          (Pax runs out, his hand to his mouth).

                        BARRY

                    (Getting up)
That's it.

                                        LIVI
Stay. He'll be *devastated* if you leave.

                                        BARRY
Devastated?
        (sitting)
Oh God.
        (gesturing toward food)
What is this?

                                        LIVI
Capon.

                                        BARRY
What?

                                        REINA
A small chicken, honey.

                                        BARRY
I know what a capon is. *Where* is it?

                                        LIVI
You have to peel it back—

                                        BARRY
(On "it") It looks like the creature from the Black Lagoon. What is this?
Algae?

                                        REINA
It's banana leaf.

                                        BARRY
(on "leaf") I know that, Reina. I'm making a joke. You know, a joke?
You know? Funny, ha ha! God. No one has any sense of humor tonight.

        (beat, he takes a bite)

                                        LIVI
Well?

                                        BARRY
Well, this is just terrible. I'm sorry, Livi.

                                        LIVI
Is it *really* that bad?

                    REINA
Yeah, Barr, maybe you're just being—

                    BARRY
Try it for yourself.
          (Beat. Reina tries it)

                    REINA
I don't know.

                    BARRY
Livi?

                    LIVI
Maybe it just needs some ketchup. I'll go get some.
          (Livi exits)

                    BARRY
What do you mean? "I don't know."

                    REINA
I'm not sure.

                    BARRY
Either you like it or you don't? How can you not be sure?

                    REINA
I'm just *not*. OK?

                    LIVI
Here we go.
          (Livi enters and puts the ketchup on the table. She adds it to
          hers, and tries the capon carefully, not sure if she likes it. Barry
          watches this, then he gets up)

                    BARRY
I can't eat this. I'm sorry, Livi.

                    LIVI
Barry...

                    BARRY
I can't *sell* this. I can't *back* this.
          (Crossing to door)
Reina.

                    REINA
Don't *bark* at me.

———
66

                              LIVI
Where are you going?

                              BARRY
Come on. We're leaving.

                              REINA
We haven't *eaten.*

                              BARRY
We'll get some dinner on the way home.

                              LIVI
You can't just *leave* like this.

                              BARRY
Just. Just tell him I re-evaluated my finances and realized I wasn't in a
position to help right now – but Reina and I really liked his food.

                              LIVI
Are you sure you can't—

                              BARRY
What else can I do? Stay and *eat* this stuff? C'mon. We'll let him down
easy. Reina.

                              REINA
Hold on, hold on, my purse.
        (She crosses to the table where she left it).

                              BARRY
You two could really use a new TV, Liv.

                              LIVI
We're *fine*, Barr.

                              BARRY
No, really. After things cool off... Have Pax stop by the Hut. I'll give
him a deal.
        (to Reina)
Got everything?

                              REINA
Yes.

                              BARRY
You have the coupons for *Steak 'n Shake* with you?

                    REINA
Always.

                    BARRY
Good. Good. OK, Livi.

          (Pax runs on)

                    PAX
SO HOW'S THE CAPE—
          (Seeing they're up)
What's going on? Why's everybody *up*?

                    LIVI
They're leaving.

                    BARRY
A family emergency.

                    REINA
Our son.

                    BARRY
He's stranded at the roller-rink.

                    PAX
Oh, but you can't go!   You haven't even tried my white chocolate plum
mousse.

                    BARRY
Well, we really have to—

                    PAX
Here. I'll just wrap everything up for you.

                    BARRY
No, that's really alright, Pax.

                    PAX
It's no problem.

                    BARRY
We don't have time. Our son *needs* us.

                    REINA
But we really enjoyed the dinner.

                    PAX
You did?

——
68

                              BARRY
Sure.

                              PAX
But you hardly *touched* it.

                              BARRY
(on "it") What we had, we liked.

                              REINA
Oh yes, Pax. Thank you so much. Just really wonderful, tasteful
cuisine. My mouth was watering the entire time. And so colorful.
Really. A great pleasure both visually and—

                              BARRY
You're *overdoing* it, Reina.

                              REINA
Well, we just really liked it, is all.
          (Pax has managed to wrap a mousse during all of this)

                              PAX
Here. A mousse for the road.
          (Reina steps forward and takes mousse from Pax)

                              REINA
I bet they'll love it in the *City of Stars*.

                              BARRY
          (Pulling Reina toward the door)
Oh, okay, well, thanks Pax.

                              REINA
Yes, thanks again, so much Pax.

                              PAX
I'm just glad you liked it.

                              BARRY
We're glad you're glad. Hey. Stop by the Techno-Hut later this week,
I'll give you a great deal on a TV.

                              PAX
Sure will, Barry. Thanks for coming over.

                              BARRY
Anytime buddy.

(Barry and Reina have sufficiently backed out of the room into the doorway, that Barry now simply closes the door as he backs the final step out and they're gone)

PAX

(Turning to Livi)
Well. That went well.

LIVI

Here, Pax, lie down on the sofa—

PAX

No, just...just eat my food, Livi. I want to *see* you eating and believing! Please.

LIVI

C'mon. Just lie down. That's good....

PAX

Barry believes!

LIVI

You have to rest now—

PAX

We can go down to the bank tomorrow and—

LIVI

No, Pax—

PAX

What do you mean, no?

LIVI

Let's get this cover around you—

PAX

Didn't you hear him? He said he loved it! This is it. This is our chance and Barry, sweet brother Barry, just gave it to us!

LIVI

No, Pax. The truth is...the truth is...

PAX

The truth is it's going to happen. Isn't it? Isn't it?
        (beat)
Isn't it?

END OF ACT ONE

———

ACT TWO

(Livi and Pax's apartment)

(Livi is pacing back and forth. Pax enters).

                    LIVI
Pax, what happened today?

                    PAX
The most incredible thing.

                    LIVI
Your boss called. He sounded angry.

                    PAX
I have something for you.

                    LIVI
He asked if you were coming in tomorrow. What was he talking about?
        (Pax takes a dress out of the box)

                    PAX
What do you think of this?

                    LIVI
It's beautiful.

                    PAX
You like it?

                    LIVI
It must have cost a fortune.

                    PAX
I spent the day trying to find the perfect one.

                    LIVI
Weren't you at work all day?

                    PAX
I liberated myself.

                    LIVI
What?

PAX

I quit.

LIVI

Why?

PAX

Let's...get you into this dress.
          (Pax begins getting Livi into the dress during the following)

LIVI

Why would you—? Are you okay?

PAX

I'm great.

LIVI

That tickles.

PAX

You're going to look amazing.

LIVI

We can't afford this. We definitely can't afford it if you quit.

PAX

Please...focus on the dress.

LIVI

This is out of our price range. This is *way* too fancy. This is...this is really nice material.

PAX

I know.

LIVI

I don't need this.

PAX

You will. For all those award ceremonies you'll be attending.

LIVI

What award ceremonies?

PAX

The Academy Awards for one.

LIVI

You're dreaming.

                         PAX
Yes.
          (Pointing at the mirror, her reflection)
Just look.

                         LIVI
          (looking at Pax)
This is silly.

                         PAX
Look at you.

          (Livi turns her body to face the mirror, but won't turn her head)
                         LIVI
I feel...

                         PAX
Look.

                         LIVI
...ridiculous...

                         PAX
You're a *vision.*

                         LIVI
          (Looks at her reflection, considering)
Am I?   ·

                         PAX
Absolutely. Imagine it. You're at the Academy Awards. You've been
nominated. In the *best actress* category. It's for some picture about
cancer and romance. You're up against Gwyneth Paltrow, Susan
Sarandon, Meryl Streep. They play your clip. You're onscreen. Pale,
wheezing, fading fast – saying goodbye to your lover. You remove...the
respirator. Ask for a final cigarette. Out of love, he grants the request.
You say something eloquent and take a drag. You both know it's your
last. His eyes well up, but you tell him he mustn't cry. You reach out to
touch his face. Two fingers extended, they run across his cheek. And
then the hand falls. And then you're gone. *Dead.* But beautifully dead.
The audience is totally devastated. The presenter can barely see
through his tears to open the envelope. "And the winner of the
Academy Award for best actress in a major motion picture...

                         LIVI
          (In her own voice, softly, almost in a trance)

                                                        73

"Livi Prichard."

                              PAX
          (To her, softly, not wanting to break the spell)
That's right. "Livi Prichard."
          (beat)
And Mr. Fine's son is going to make that happen for you. And guess
what? Today, I met someone who can help me. Who *will* help me.

                              LIVI
Who?

                              PAX
She came into the Steak 'n Shake today. She's a businesswoman.

                              LIVI
Today? What kind of business?

                              PAX
Dream-making. She wants mine to come true.

                              LIVI
Why?

                              PAX
Because she tried my tuna.

                              LIVI
Your tuna?

                              PAX
My Ahi tuna. Yes.

                              LIVI
At the Steak 'n Shake?

                              PAX
There was something *about* her, Livi. Something almost other-worldly.
She had this glow to her skin. This brightness about her. She wore this
intense, white silk suit.

                              LIVI
She didn't belong there.

                              PAX
No, she was completely out of her element. She looked tired and
hungry. She ordered the tuna melt. And as she raised the plate to her
nose to smell it, she began to look very ill. Her whole hue started to
change, to darken...

(Beat)

And it was like, and I know this sounds crazy but, it was like she was...calling to me. To *nourish* her. I...I stop flipping burgers. I go to her. I tell her I'll make her something better. She just smiles at me. This weird, knowing smile. I send the busboy to the little Japanese market down the way for the Ahi and some spices. And I make her the tuna, like I made it for you on our first date. I bring it to her and she begins to eat it. With every bite, it's like she's getting brighter and brighter until it's almost hard to look at her and then she asks me – she says "what is it you want?" with this incredible warmth. I tell her all about "The Garden." Turns out, *she's* from the City of Stars. She said she'd be interested in *helping* me if I came out there—

LIVI

What's her name?

(Beat)

PAX

Her name is Hope.

LIVI

Hope?

PAX

Hope.

LIVI

Does she have a last name?

PAX

She just goes by Hope. I know it's a little hard to believe....

LIVI

A *little* hard to believe?

PAX

Why can't you be happy for me? And excited for us? I mean, don't you see *now* we can both go out there. I have Hope, you have Mr. Fine's son—

LIVI

But I *don't.*

PAX

Sure, he said you have a *unique look.*

LIVI

Mr. Fine's son is in jail.

PAX

What?

LIVI

One of the Care Aid's cousins lives in Hollywood – it was all over the
news there...

PAX

What was?

LIVI

He was making porn films, Pax. Some of the girls were underage...

PAX

But his connections at William Morris—

LIVI

QUIT DREAMING! He never *worked* for William Morris.

PAX

That's okay. It doesn't matter. Hope is very connected out there.
She'll help you too. It's a miracle. Hope has granted us a chance. But
we have to go to the City of Stars. It can only happen in the City of
Stars. And I...I need you to believe me.

LIVI

But Pax...

PAX

Yes?

LIVI

I don't.

SCENE 2:

(Barry and Reina's bedroom)

(The music from *2001* plays. Reina enters, wearing an astronaut
uniform. It's a dreamy moment as she "flies" around the room,
imagining. She stops in front of a mirror to admire her "astronaut self."
Barry enters, watches for a moment, then uses the remote to turn off
the stereo, music stops)

BARRY

Where'd you get that?

                         REINA

Costume shop.

                         BARRY

Rented?
        (Reina doesn't answer. She continues to pose in the mirror)
No? You *bought* that?

                         REINA

Shhh.

                         BARRY

How? With what money?
        (Looking through his wallet)
You stole my credit card?

                         REINA

Borrowed.

                         BARRY

Well. Give it to me!

                         REINA

It's in my purse.

        (Barry goes and roughly empties the contents of her purse and
        gets his card, replacing it in his wallet. He does not put the
        contents of her purse back)

                         BARRY

I can't believe this. You *stole* from me. Did I tell you that you could just
take my credit card?

                         REINA

(over "my credit card") I'm sick of always having to *beg* you for
everything.

                         BARRY

You could have just *asked.*

                         REINA

You would have said no. You *always* say no.

                         BARRY

I swear to you. Next time you pull something like this...

                         REINA

Don't threaten me.   You know, Robert says that in a healthy
relationship each partner has some level of financial <u>independence.</u>

BARRY

Well, maybe if you tried for a job other than *astronaut...*

REINA

Robert thinks that maybe some of our problems in bed are due to you not allowing me financial independence.

BARRY

I'm paying for you to go to *Robert's* class, so he can say these things?

REINA

Oh, it's not just him saying it. He read about it in *Woman Magazine.*

BARRY

He reads *Woman Magazine*?

REINA

He says his mother keeps a stack in the bathroom.

BARRY

He lives with his mother?

REINA

He was *visiting.* You're missing the point!

BARRY

Which is I should just freely *give* you my money...

REINA

Yes.

BARRY

So we can have sex again?

REINA

(Weakly)
Uh-huh.

BARRY

Seems to me *Woman Magazine* is promoting some kind of weird marital prostitution.

REINA

No. No. It's a question of *equality.* Of partners feeling *equal.*

BARRY

Remind me never to give you money for that *Woman Magazine*.
    (Beat)

What? I'm kidding. How much it cost? Three dollars? You want three dollars? Here.
>(Extends hand with money. Reina doesn't take it. Barry takes it back)
Look. Just don't steal from me.

                              REINA
I'm your wife!

SCENE 3:

(Livi and Pax's Apartment)

(The couch is covered with Pax's things. Books, clothes, pots, pans.
Pax enters with an armful of their possessions. Livi is right behind him)

                              LIVI
We can't just leave.
>(Pax exits)
We can't just take off like this. Like two thieves in the night—

                              PAX
>(offstage)
We got married that way.

                              LIVI
I want you to call Reina back. Tell her she doesn't have to come over. I mean. We can't just go. We don't even have a way to get there.

                              PAX
>(enters with another armful of possession)
The bus.

                              LIVI
We can't take all this on a bus.

                              PAX
Don't have to. We'll store it at my parents' house. Just have to get it packed up. I already bought the bus tickets. See.
>(Pax hands the tickets to her and exits, she looks at the tickets)

                              LIVI
This is nuts. I don't even know that this Hope woman is real.
>(She puts the tickets down on the coffee table)

(Pax enters with a few empty cardboard boxes)

                              PAX

She is.

                              LIVI
Like your big brother Bret?

                              PAX
This isn't the same thing.

                              LIVI
How do I know?

                              PAX
Hope has a distinctive look, Livi – I'm sure someone else at the Steak 'n Shake noticed her.

                              LIVI
So if I called the Steak 'n Shake, someone would back your story?

                              PAX
Of course.

                              LIVI
So I can just go ahead and call then.

                              PAX
Go for it.

                              LIVI
It wouldn't be a problem if I called to check your story?

                              PAX
No.

                              LIVI
I'm going to call.

                              PAX
Fine.
        (Doorbell rings)
Could you get the door first?

                              LIVI
Why can't you?

                              PAX
(over "you') I'm a bit occupied at the moment.
        (Pax exits. Livi goes to the door, opens it. Reina, still in her
        astronaut suit, enters).

———

                              LIVI
Hi Reina.

                              REINA
          (Seeing the boxes, clothes and belongings strewn about)
What's going on?

                              LIVI
Wish I knew.

                              REINA
Pax called and I came. Something about helping with packing?

                              LIVI
He wants us to move.

                              REINA
Move? Really? When?

                              LIVI
Tonight, I guess.

                              REINA
Where to?

                              LIVI
L.A.

                              REINA
The City of Stars! That's wonderful.
          (beat)
That's a beautiful dress.

                              LIVI
Thank you. May I ask...what...what are you wearing?

                              REINA
Do you like it? I'm practicing for life as an astronaut.

                              LIVI
Oh.

                              REINA
NASA's response should be coming in the mail any day now. If I'm
accepted I want to be ready, you know? I'm pre-visualizing, getting into
the zone, seeing myself as ASTRONAUT REINA!

                              LIVI
Mmmm.

                    REINA
But I'm also so excited for you two. Running off to follow your dreams.
Give me a hug.

                    LIVI
(over "Give me a hug") Actually, I'm not sure that we're really going
to—
            (Pax enters with another armful of things)

                    PAX
Reina! Thanks for coming.

                    REINA
Oh sure. I was just telling Livi how excited I am for you both.

                    PAX
Yeah, it's finally happening!
            (Livi starts to exit)
Livi, where are you going?

                    LIVI
To make that call.

                    PAX
But we'll need your help packing if we're going to get out of here
tonight. We really don't have time to—
            (Livi is gone)

                    REINA
Everything okay?

                    PAX
She's a little nervous, is all. Let's start getting this stuff in boxes.

                    REINA
Right.
            (They begin loading items into the boxes)

                    PAX
Practicing to be an astronaut, huh?

                    REINA
How did you know?

                    PAX
I did the same thing. Walked around in a chef's hat when I first started
dreaming about it back in college.

                              REINA

Between you and me...sometimes I feel a little silly. At the grocery
store today, people were looking at me like I was crazy.

                              PAX

Let them look. None of them have the courage to dream so *openly*...

                              REINA

Yeah...

                              PAX

Really. You have something they wish they had. A spark.

                              REINA

You really think I have a spark?

                              PAX

Of course. I saw it the day you read that course description.

                              REINA

Oh yeah. It's a great class.

                              PAX

I'll bet.

                              REINA

Robert is teaching me all kinds of things. Like cities among the stars
can be anything we want them to be. For example: think of your
perfect world.

                              PAX

Now?

                              REINA

Yes, close your eyes and see it.

                              PAX

Okay.

                              REINA

Are you seeing it?

                              PAX

Yes. Do you want me to share it?

                              REINA

Well, you don't have to—

                              PAX

I'm naked. Everyone is naked and happy. There's incredible food all around us. I've cooked it all. Livi is there. She's singing "The Hills Are Alive."

                              REINA
Oh, she was great in *The Sound of Music*—

                              PAX
Yeah... Wow. That was a rush. That was great.

                              REINA
See. You can have that in space "without the dirty old world interfering," as Robert says. You can make any world you want out there and populate it with whomever you please.

                              PAX
Huh. Space.
          (laughing)
Maybe we'll try that if L.A. doesn't work out.

                              REINA
You should! It'd be great to have you and Livi in space with me.

                              PAX
You're great, Reina. Really, no holds barred.

                              REINA
I'm just so happy.

                              PAX
I can see that.
          (beat)
Houston to Reina. Houston to Reina, let's keep packing.
          (They pack for a few moments in silence)
Reina...

                              REINA
Yeah?

                              PAX
It's not always *easy.* You know?

                              REINA
I know.

                              PAX
I mean. Keeping the spark going. Even when the world says... "no," you have to be able to tell yourself "yes" and keep pushing on.

———

REINA

Not so easy, is it?

PAX .

No.

(Beat)

REINA

Hey. Let me buy you and Livi dinner?

PAX

Oh, that's alright—

REINA

No, really, I mean... Barry gave me his credit card and...it looks like
we're going to be here awhile... plus, the last time, *you* treated *me* so...

PAX

I just don't think that's necessary.

REINA

(over "necessary") You like fancy food, right? I'll order dinner from
somewhere fancy.   Where's the phone?

PAX

Livi's got it in her room. But you really don't have to—

REINA

Let me do something for you.

(beat)

PAX

I guess you can go see if she's done with the phone.

REINA

Great! I'll be quick and then we can keep packing.

PAX

Thanks, Reina.
(Reina exits. Pax is alone for a moment. He takes a big breath.
And keeps packing. After a moment, Reina enters, phone in
hand)

REINA

I think she finished making her call.

PAX

Is she okay?

                    REINA

She's crying.

                     PAX

I'd better look in on her.

                    REINA

I'll....order dinner...

          (Pax exits)

          (Reina rifles through the yellow pages, looking for a place to
          order from. She finds a number)

                    REINA
Yes, hello. I'd like to order the fanciest thing you have on your menu.
You *do* have a delivery service, correct? Perfect.

                     PAX
          (offstage)
Livi talk to me. Say something. Where are you going?
          (Livi storms into the living room)

                    REINA
Now what *is* the fanciest thing on your menu?
          (Pax enters)

                     PAX

What's wrong? *Talk* to me.

                    REINA
Filet minions sound good.   Are you two okay with filet minions?
          (Note: Reina pronounces filet mignon incorrectly, as filet
          minions. Minions as in "minions of evil")

                     LIVI

This whole dream is a lie.

                    REINA

Oh, sorry. Filet mignons.

                     PAX

It's not. We'll make it out there.

                    REINA

We'll take three.

———

                         LIVI
How? How will we?

                         PAX
Hope will help.

                         REINA
My credit card? It's a Visa.

                         LIVI
She doesn't *exist*.

                         REINA
The name on the card is Barry James.
          (During the following Reina gives her credit card info)

                         PAX
You have to have faith.

                         LIVI
No one at the Steak 'n Shake remembers her.

                         PAX
No one?

                         LIVI
I must have talked to twelve employees. Not one person remembers
seeing the woman you described.

                         PAX
Did you talk to...?

                         LIVI
Who?

                         REINA
What do you mean it was reported stolen? No. That can't be right.
There must be some mistake. Well, run it through again.

                         LIVI
(Over "No. That can't be right.") Did I talk to who?

                         PAX
To Carl. The busboy. He's the one who got the Ahi for me. He
definitely saw her.

                         LIVI
He did?

                              PAX
Talk to the busboy Carl.

                              LIVI
I don't know, Pax...

                              PAX
I can't do this without you.

                              LIVI
Fine. I'll make one more phone call. But this is the last one.

                              REINA
No, I am not a thief, how dare you call me a... I'm his wife! I'm Barry
James' wife! I'm Reina James! Please. All I want is three filet mignons.
Please. Don't hang up. Please. I have another one of his credit cards
on me, I... Hello? Hello? Hello?
        (She puts the phone down)
I feel so... I'm sorry. I'll try to come back and help, but, right now... I
can't...

SCENE 4:

(Barry and Reina's Bedroom)

(Lights come up on Barry in his bed, watching TV – he's having a great
time. Reina storms in, credit card in one hand)

                              REINA
I cannot *believe* you did that to me!

              (Reina throws the credit card at Barry. Barry begins chuckling.
              This builds to an all-out guffawing during the following)

                              REINA
I was completely humiliated. I mean, to sit there on the phone and be
treated like a *criminal.*

                              BARRY
I told you, if you stole my card again—

                              REINA
I just wanted to treat Livi and Pax for once. For once I wanted to be the
one *paying*—

                              BARRY
It was *me,* paying. Well, in this case, actually...*it wasn't.*
        (laughs harder)

———

88

REINA

Stop that! Just stop that laughing right now! You are such a slimy, forked-tongued—

BARRY

Hey, *I'm* not the one who *lied*—

REINA

YOU ARE THE BIGGEST ASSHOLE ON THE PLANET!
        (Beat. Barry holds up a letter from NASA)
Jesus.
        (Getting more and more excited and worried)
Jesus. Jesus. Jesus. Jesus.
        (beat)

BARRY

Jesus.

REINA

The envelope's kinda thin. That's bad. Right? I mean. That's kinda bad, isn't it?

BARRY

Just open it, Rey.

REINA

I mean. It might not be. Bad. Right? How many pages do they really need to say: "congratulations, you're in." Right?

BARRY

I'm sure they *interview*, Rey.

REINA

I mean. Right! Interview. Exactly! How many pages does it take to tell you you're a *finalist?* Right?
        (beat)
This could be *good.* Right?

BARRY

I... I don't know.

REINA

You don't *care.*

BARRY

Why don't you just *open* it!

REINA

Just open it? *Just* open it? I can't *just* open it. This envelope is *everything.* My *life* is inside this envelope.

                    BARRY
You want me to open it?

                    REINA
Don't touch it. This is my envelope. You just get away from my envelope.

                    BARRY
Fine. Whatever.

                    REINA
"Whatever?" "WHATEVER!?"

                    BARRY
What? What did I say?

        (Reina goes to begin opening it. Stops).

                    REINA
You. You've been against this from the beginning. You don't want there to be good news inside this. You'd love it if I opened it and failed. Because you don't want an astronaut wife! You don't want Cities in the Stars! YOU CAN'T EVEN FATHOM THE IDEA!

                    BARRY
JUST OPEN IT!

                    REINA
YOU WITH ALL YOUR STUPID SALESMAN *BULLSHIT,* COULDN'T BEGIN TO COMPREHEND WHAT I'M TRYING TO DO—

                    BARRY
GIVE ME THIS!
        (He snatches the envelope)

                    REINA
Barry, no!

        (They do a cat and mouse around the bed)

BARRY
You don't *think* I *understand* what you're trying to *do* with this?
        (on "this" he shakes the envelope in his hand)

                    REINA
Barry!

———

90

BARRY

This big *noble* thing you want to do for humanity—

REINA

(over "humanity") Give it!

BARRY

You think it's way above a Techno-Hut salesman's head? Right? Look, I get it *because* I'm a Techno-Hut salesman! I see all this technology all day long; and I think if we can create something as amazing as a fifty-inch flat screen plasma television, just imagine what we could do if we really pooled our resources and got focused.

REINA

Give me the envelope.

BARRY

I mean, why are we wasting our time fighting amongst ourselves? That's Robert's whole point. Right? RIGHT?

REINA

I swear to God, Barry—

BARRY

You know why human beings are constantly fighting instead of working together to survive? I'll tell you why!

REINA

Oh yeah, *you'll* tell me. Just give me my—

BARRY

It's the same motivation that made man invent the fifty-inch plasma TV. Man is essentially motivated, *primarily* motivated to <u>sit on his ass</u>.

REINA

Brilliant, Barry. You should teach a course at community college.

BARRY

You wanted me to talk about this stuff. I'm talking about it! Men kill for their right to sit on their ass. I'm telling you, wars happen because every man wants the best Lazy Boy Recliner in the galaxy to relax on.

REINA

No, they don't.

BARRY

AND WE HAVE IT AT TECHNO-HUT.

REINA

IF YOU OPEN THAT—!

BARRY

See we have this automated Lazy Boy. This super deluxe Lazy Boy is outfitted with massagers, heating pads, a cooling unit for drinks – it's the closest experience of comfort a man can get on earth short of climbing back through his mother's vagina back up into her womb!

REINA

OH, COME ON. What are you even saying—

BARRY

I'm saying we as a race of beings are still in our infancy. Clinging to our collective womb. And while we try to stay in our infancy, so we create and... *perpetuate* a global infancy filled with global temper tantrums. AND THAT'S JUST THE WAY IT IS!

REINA

IT DOESN'T HAVE TO BE THAT WAY. WE CAN GROW UP. We can grow up.

BARRY

Not gonna happen.

REINA

Don't you want it to?

BARRY

It's just a *dream*. It's a dream to think we'll get our collective ass in gear and get motivated by something besides finding more ways to sit on our ass better. I mean, technologically speaking, we're on the cusp of it. We *could* become truly independent.

REINA

Yes!

BARRY

But first we'd have to decide. Do we want world peace and a chance at long-term perpetuation of humankind, or do we want the Lazy Boy Recliner?
        (beat)
I *work* at the Techno-Hut. Every year, I meet thousands of *representative* members of human kind. And I *know* what they want. I give them what they want.

REINA

No. You're tempting them. With your apple pie *a' la mode* and your fancy gadgets, you're cheating them out of their chance at a better life, and a better world.

    (beat)

                    BARRY
I only offer them the choice, Reina.
    (He hands her the envelope).

    (Reina opens the envelope and begins reading it).

SCENE 5:

(Pax and Livi's Apartment)

(Pax stands, nervously watching the entrance to the bedroom. Livi enters, phone in hand)

                    PAX
So? What'd you find out?

                    LIVI
The busboy no longer works at the Steak 'n Shake. He quit....to pursue a PhD in anthropology.

                    PAX
Not surprised. That busboy was always interested in people.

                    LIVI
Okay, but he can't corroborate your story—

                    PAX
(over "your story") He proves it though, doesn't he? That Hope exists.

                    LIVI
How does he prove—

                    PAX
Hope must be helping him too.

                    LIVI
To get a PhD in Anthropology?

                    PAX
She's very connected. I have something for you to try.
    (He exits)

                         LIVI
What are you doing?

                         PAX
        (offstage)
I made them this morning. They're best hot, but they're not bad chilled
either.
        (Pax enters, with a plate of tapas in hand)

                         LIVI
What are those?

                         PAX
Tapas. Garlicky eggplant and tomato tapas. One taste of these and
you'll know we can make it out there.

                         LIVI
This is silly.

                         PAX
Taste my tapas.

                         LIVI
I'm not hungry.

                         PAX
Taste my tapas!

                         LIVI
Not right now.

                         PAX
TASTE MY TAPAS!

                         LIVI
FINE! I'll get the ketchup.

                         PAX
They're no good with ketchup. You have to try them pure.
        (She's almost at the kitchen, but is stopped by...)
You're so scared.

                         LIVI
I'm not...

                         PAX
You're even scared to *say* you're scared.

                         LIVI

I am not...

                    PAX
Say it! Say "I'm scared!" I'm scared of taking a risk on my dreams!
I'm scared of my husband's dreams! I'm scared to death! I'm even
terrified of a little tapa!

                    LIVI
This is childish. I'm not going to eat this just to prove something to you.

                    PAX
Livi, I'm trying to help us – get us free, really free – really. There's a
horrible gravity to this place. I'm afraid if we don't get out soon...

                    LIVI
Pax even if we go...the chances of us making it out there...

                    PAX
You know how the coyote used to run over the chasm while chasing the
roadrunner—

                    LIVI
What?

                    PAX
He'd run and run over the empty chasm and only when he looked down,
realized the impossibility of what he was doing...only *then* would he
fall—but what if he kept running instead...would he have made it?

                    LIVI
We're not cartoons! We're people who have to face the reality that the
majority of restaurants fail, and the majority of actors are out of work—
the truth is—

                    PAX
You looked down. You keep looking down.

                    LIVI
I keep facing facts.

                    PAX
We don't need to. We've got Hope.

                    LIVI
Where? Where is she? I want to see her. We've got *vapors.* We've got
some elusive, ephemeral fantasy of a chance—

                    PAX
You're miserable here.

                              LIVI
I am useful here. I spend my days *tending* to the needs of the needy—

                              PAX
What about your own needs?

                              LIVI
You're enough for me, Pax. Why can't I be enough for you.

                              PAX
I want us to be happy.

                              LIVI
We can be happy here. Let's stay.

                              PAX
Let's go.

                              LIVI
Where are you trying to run to, Pax? Can't you just stop and enjoy life
while you're here—lucky to be alive and breathing? I mean, there may
be no tomorrow and you may have missed today in some desperate,
frenetic, striving frenzy. I like the people at the home. Their time is
limited and they know it. They have a palpable sense of their limits.
And they know how to enjoy the moment. There's an old couple there,
that I aspire to. They sit together, all day, hand in hand, just breathing,
staring at the TV.

                              PAX
Like...just two bodies...sitting there?

                              LIVI
Yes.

                              PAX
A sitting-down love?

                              LIVI
Yes.

                              PAX
Love should make you stand up, jump up...achieve your greatest
heights.

                              LIVI
It should make you calm, centered, at peace, contented.

———

                              PAX
Is that really what you want for us? A life in retirement?

                              LIVI
I want us to be fulfilled.

                              PAX
So do I.

                              LIVI
Then accept things the way they are.

                              PAX
Just give up?

                              LIVI
Give in.

                              PAX
Accept death.

                              LIVI
No matter how fast you run, you can't outrun it.

                              PAX
We can try. We can fly on the stars and never look back.

                              LIVI
Sometimes falling can feel like flying.

                              PAX
Falling?

                              LIVI
Through thin air...and doggie paddling like mad—

                              PAX
That's not what we'd be doing. We both have real propulsion, real talent.
We can both take off, if you'll let us. You're so scared. You're
paralyzed, Livi. Isn't that the truth? Isn't *that* the only truth that
matters?
        (beat)
Hold on, I've got it! There *was* a moment when you believed, when he
smiled at you, and you believed...it's the missing piece! The catalyst!
        (Pax exits to the bedroom at a run)

                              LIVI
What are you doing?

(NOTE: The action of Scene 5 continues into Scene 6 in bold font. We are seeing both couples at their respective locations)

SCENE 6:

(Barry and Reina's Bedroom)

(Barry enters, Steak 'n Shake to-go bags in hand, Reina enters with a few items of clothing, a small suitcase is open on the bed).

                              BARRY
          (in a sing song voice, shaking the bags)
Look what I brought! (words drawn out playfully: looook what Aiyeeeee braawwwwt!)
          (Seeing the suitcase)
What's going on?

                              REINA
I'm still going!

                              BARRY
What do you mean? You didn't get in!

(Pax comes back in, with Livi's tiara)

                              PAX
Put it on.

                              REINA
Sometimes when the world tells you "no," you have to tell yourself "yes."

                              BARRY
What?

                              PAX
Go on.
          (She puts it on)

                              REINA
I'm going to go to NASA!   I know once they *see* me in person, *talk* to me... I have a spark!

                              BARRY
Calm down.

                              PAX

98

Now look at that girl in the mirror and tell me – honestly – that she doesn't have more than just a vapor of a chance.

                    REINA
I'm going to NASA Headquarters.

                    BARRY
Jesus. That's all the way in D.C., you know that, right?

                    LIVI
This is silly.

                    REINA
Of course I know that.

                    LIVI
I feel like a child playing dress-up.

                    BARRY
How are you getting there?

                    PAX
That's just how you *should* feel.   Like a child!

                    REINA
I'll get there.

                    BARRY
How?

                    PAX
As children we're filled with this sense of unbounded, unabashed joy.

                    REINA
Pax and Livi will take me on their way to The City of Stars.

                    PAX
And if we're not careful—

                    BARRY
What?

                    PAX
The need to be "realistic" and "adult" will bash the unabashed joy right out of us.

                    REINA
The City of Stars is L.A.

BARRY

We're in the Midwest!   D.C. isn't even on the way to L.A.

REINA

Then they'll drop me at the Kennedy Space Center.

BARRY

That's in Florida!

PAX

You still have your spark – that little part of you that experiences true, unabashed joy is still intact.   But I'm afraid for it. That's why we need to go, Livi. *Now.*

REINA

I'm going.

LIVI

You really think I have a spark?

PAX

Yes, a spark, we both have it, Livi...

BARRY

What'll you do when you get there?

PAX

...but it's endangered...

BARRY

Who will even talk to you there – at NASA?

PAX

...dreamers like us, we're an endangered species, and the only way we can escape extinction...is to keep dreaming.

REINA

I'm going.

BARRY

You really think the head of admissions is going to talk to you? They have hundreds of applicants....

REINA

I'm going.

LIVI

And if I stop dreaming....?

(Livi begins to take off the dress as...)

(Barry moves behind Reina, and begins to take off the astronaut costume)

(Both women are facing into opposite sides of a stand-up mirror, in their respective homes as they are "stripped" of their dreams)

REINA

What are you doing?

PAX
(Simultaneous to Reina's "What are you doing") No.

BARRY

Shhh. Just relax now.

LIVI
If I accept the natural course of my life—

REINA

I can't...

PAX

This isn't natural, this is—

BARRY

It's okay, honey.

LIVI
Then I go...go...extinct?

(Barry finishes taking off Reina's astronaut costume at the same time as
(Livi finishes taking off her dress and removes the tiara).

LIVI
Let's go to bed.

PAX
You want us to just...turn in?   To retire?

LIVI
Just for tonight.

PAX
For forever. You mean for forever, don't you?

LIVI

Come to bed.

(Livi exits to bedroom. Pax watches after her a moment, then walks quickly into the bedroom after her)

(Barry and Reina both are in bed now. After a few moments).

BARRY

Look....   I'm... I'm sorry you didn't get in.

REINA

Yeah.

BARRY

What do you need to be an astronaut for anyway, huh? Space? Who needs it? Right? That's sci-fi. Stuff for dreamers. I mean, what are they escaping? Where are they trying to get to? Look around our bedroom. State-of-the-art, Techno-Hut adjustable bed, surround-sound speaker system, a nice big high-definition television. This is it. The American Dream. The best destination anyone could hope for. We've *arrived.*

(Reina looks around, lost, even a little frightened, as Barry turns on the TV).

(Blackout on Barry and Reina scene)

SCENE 7:

(Pax and Livi's Apartment)

(Pax comes out of the bedroom, carrying a backpack, Livi follows after him)

PAX

I have to go to the City of Stars tonight, Liv.

LIVI

No.

PAX

Last bus leaves in a few minutes.

LIVI

This isn't fair. You have to at least wait till tomorrow.   Just—

PAX

I might never leave, I wait till tomorrow.

                              LIVI
You can't go. You need me to believe.

                              PAX
But Livi...

                              LIVI
Yes?

                              PAX
You don't.
          (He turns to leave)

                              LIVI
Okay. OKAY!
          (He stops for a moment)
If you stay another day. I'll try it. Anything and everything on your
menu. *No* ketchup. *No* Thousand Island...

                              PAX
Too late. And I can't afford to believe you.
          (Beat. He picks up her bus ticket off the coffee table and hands
          it to her)
But here. Your bus ticket. Just in case.

                              LIVI
This is crazy. I have no way to verify that Hope exists.

                              PAX
You come with me. You could meet her. Really get to *know* her. She'll
be our best friend out there.

                              LIVI
I'm not even packed.

                              PAX
Take the leap.

                              LIVI
One more dinner. Please.

                              PAX
(over "please") I *can't.*

                              LIVI
I'll try it. I promise.

                              PAX

You promise?

                    LIVI
Yes.
        (They kiss)

                    PAX
Okay. Okay! But no dinner – you try these tapas, right now.

                    LIVI
Art meant to be devoured. Right?

                    PAX
Right.

                    LIVI
What's in this again?

                    PAX
It's a surprise. Go on. It's good. I promise.

                    LIVI
I want to.

                    PAX
We'll cook these up all the time at The Garden. We could do a cabaret
Saturdays. Serve these as appetizers—

                    LIVI
A dinner theatre.

                    PAX
Until you made it big.

                    LIVI
I'm afraid.

                    PAX
I know.
        (Beat. Looking at his watch. Urgent)
Livi...we've got to go! The bus!

                    LIVI
What if this isn't...

        (She looks at the tapa in the plate on her lap)

                    PAX

Go on, Livi. One *real* taste. And then you'll believe. And then you can come.

> (She continues to stare down at her lap, at the food. Unable to move. Pax looks at his watch, and watches her a few more moments. Quietly he gets his things and goes. Several moments pass. Livi, unaware, slowly picks up the tapa and tries it. It takes a moment to sink in and then).

LIVI

It's good.
> (She looks around, realizing he's gone. Calling after him)
Pax, it's good! It's good! It's good! Pax. Pax!
> (Quietly, to herself)
It's good.

> (She looks at the bus ticket in her hand, and then in the direction in which he left. She quickly sits, and tensely, trying to decide if she should go after him. She rocks back and forth, full of energy – excited, but also anxious – on the verge of taking action. The sound of the bus departing can be heard as we fade to black)

END OF PLAY